Learn
Home Staging

A Complete Course Created by Adam Rostocki:
Author of Home-Staging-Home-Stager.Com

INTRODUCTION

Welcome to my easy guide on home staging. My name is Adam Rostocki and I am an independent home staging consultant working in New York City and Long Island, NY. It is my goal to help you attain all the basic skills needed to integrate home staging into your real estate business, stage your own house for sale or begin a new career as a professional home stager. The material in this book is supplemented by the many articles on my website: home-staging-home-stager.com

I highly recommend you utilize the material on the website to increase your knowledge and understanding of real estate staging. The site is always free and is updated regularly, so check back often for the latest offerings in the world of property enhancement and marketing.

This easy-to-follow book is a self contained course on the basics of home staging. The book contains all the information you ever need to successfully achieve any of the following objectives:

- Get started on a new career in home staging
- Add basic staging services to your real estate business
- Research home staging for personal or professional projects
- Hire a home stager to prepare your house for sale
- Stage your own home for sale

I became seriously interested in home staging in 2003, when I was getting ready to sell my first home. I had bought the property three years prior and had renovated it lovingly myself. Luckily I had the construction and design skills to do all the work, saving me a tremendous amount of cash, compared to the price of professional contracting.

When I spoke to a local real estate expert about listing the home, he assured me that the price I wanted was way too high. He asked me to drop the price by $35,000 and list with him. Although this guy was considered the king of real estate in my area, I knew something he apparently did not. I knew how I could make my home show much stronger than he thought possible. I knew the all about the power of home staging. I explained my theory to him, but he dismissed it and told me to call him when and if I came to my senses. I was truly motivated now to succeed in getting my asking price...

I went about doing what I knew was right and developed a look and feel for the home that I was confident would appeal to virtually all prospective buyers. The house was old and had many problematic issues. However, it was in a great neighborhood and I knew that I could make it look like a showplace.

I staged the entire home, using my own existing furnishings and a few newly purchased items, for a total cost of less than $400. The home looked fabulous and I knew it was ready to go. I found a different real estate agent who loved the home and listed it at the price I desired.

Well, vindication is certainly sweet, but I do not want to gloat. The home sold after being on the market for only 3 days, for <u>full asking price</u>. The selling price was almost double what I had paid for the home just 3 years before. This gave me all the confidence I needed to further investigate the power of property staging and set my path on a new and exciting career.

I hope that you will enjoy this book and will be able to utilize it successfully in fulfilling all your home staging aspirations.

- Adam Rostocki

SECTION ONE:

What is Home Staging?

Home staging: Most of us have heard the term, but many people still do not understand the exact definition of the words. In order to clarify what home staging is, please bear with me while I tell you what it isn't. Home staging is <u>not</u> decorating. Home staging is <u>not</u> renovation. Home staging is <u>not</u> performed to suit the décor preferences of the home owner. Home staging is <u>not</u> inherently expensive. Home staging is <u>not</u> a luxury or frivolous option.

Ok, let's move on to what home staging really is:

Home staging is also known as property staging, real estate staging or home fluffing. Staging describes methods of preparing real estate, residential or commercial, for sale or rental, by creating an atmosphere of universal appeal inside and outside the property.

Home staging is a solution used by any property seller to increase the likelihood of receiving one or more lucrative offers on their real estate offerings. Home staging is the best way to invest money in a home in order to maximize profitability from the sale. In a nutshell, property staging is all about selling homes faster and for a higher price, thereby making more money from the sale and freeing the owner up to move on to their new home.

Real estate staging can be confusing to some, since they simply view it as decorating or interior design. However, it is very different, often not in the actual changes made to a property, but instead, for the reasons why the changes are made. Decorating and interior design seeks to fulfill the needs and wants of the present homeowner. They are used to better suit the preferences of the family currently occupying the home.

Staging is exactly the opposite. Property staging seeks to create an atmosphere which will appeal to prospective buyers. In order to do so, the stylistic footprint of the current owner must be drastically reduced or removed, so that buyers can envision themselves living happily in the home.

Staging works through various processes and components. Staging can be used for any type of real estate and can facilitate a sale or rental to a general market or a particular segment of property consumers.

Using this guide, you will come to understand home staging in all its forms and will be able to implement staging as part of your own real estate marketing strategy. You may even decide that you want to pursue staging as a career path, since the opportunities are better than ever and the industry is growing at a phenomenal rate. Ok, let's begin...

Home Staging Basics

The primary purpose of home staging is to make a piece of property more desirable to prospective buyers. This is accomplished by improving the look, feel and flow of the interior of the home, as well as enhancing the curb appeal and landscaping on the exterior of the home.

Staging seeks to remove the present owner's style and personality from the home and replace it with furniture, art and accessories which have a more universal appeal. Staging consists of altering many possible characteristics of the home, including color palate, style, proportion, architectural details, layout and functionality.

What Exactly is "Universal Appeal"?

Staging is known for trying to appeal to the aesthetic sensibilities, functional needs, preferences and tastes of the "target buyer". This is the definition of universal appeal. In essence, it means to alter the property to stop representing the stylistic tastes of the owner and allow it to represent to want lists of likely potential buyers.

A target buyer or target demographic is the type of person or family that is most likely to purchase the home. While there is no way of knowing for certain who the eventual buyer will be, the home is likely to be actively marketed towards a particular demographic. Some of these target groups include:

* First time buyers
* Trade up buyers
* Luxury home buyers
* Large family buyers
* Single buyers
* Young buyers
* Empty nesters

Making the home fulfill the want-lists of the target demographic will create universal appeal, enacting the ideal circumstances for a fast and profitable sale!

Distinction

Most buyers will see many homes before making a choice on the best property for their needs. Often, they will spend hours at a time viewing properties, which can be a daunting and confusing task. It is very easy to get the details of one home switched with the details of another. Many buyers take written notes, which helps to keep the homes in accurate perspective, but some of the fine points are bound to be lost in the recesses of an over-burdened memory.

Home staging helps to distinguish a property from its competition using beautiful designs which are memorable. Additionally, property staging is performed with the intention of calling buyer attention to the best features of a home, while distracting from less desirable aspects. This will not only leave a clear mental picture of a staged home in potential buyers' minds, but will also enrich the written notes they take about the property. Once they go home after seeing 3, 6 or 10 properties, the staged property will be the one which will stand out in their mind.

Optimization

How often do buyers speculate about the "potential" of a home? In my business, it is everyday. Potential basically means that the current décor and set-up may be a complete disaster, but with some fixing, the home could be nice. This thought pattern is an extension of every buyer's inner need to disconnect the property from the current owner and connect it to their own life. Potential is another way of saying...

"I think I can make this house work... I hope...I pray..."

<u>Potential is a form of compromise.</u>

Buyers will settle for compromise if they have no choice, but this decision will take time and an exhaustive search for available properties before it becomes reality. Why make a buyer settle for anything? Home staging is all about optimizing any home to appeal to buyers right now. When prospective buyers see a fully staged home, they will certainly not say,

"This house has potential."

Instead, they will say, "<u>This house is perfect</u>".

The reason for this fact is simple. Home staging has already acted on the home's potential, taking the "could be good" out of the equation and replacing it with a definitive "is already ideal".

Other Staging Fine Points

Many people argue that...

"Buyers are looking at my home, not my stuff or my style".

Real estate sales statistics prove this to be completely untrue. While it is sensible to understand that the way a home is decorated, set-up and maintained has little to do with the property itself, buyers simply can not help but become emotionally involved in the things they see in every home they are considering.

Here are some of the other main goals of home staging and how they relate to fulfilling a buyer's demanding wish list:

- Organization is crucial. Messy, cluttered and disorganized spaces are difficult to view and make the entire house look ill kept. Buyers will judge the seller and their ability to keep a nice home by the manner in which their personal possessions are arranged, displayed and stored. Staging will declutter spaces and arrange the remaining furnishings aesthetically.

- Personal possessions are a distraction to buyers who tend to gravitate towards the "back story" of the owner, rather than focus on the home itself. This is a fundamental problem. Therefore, staging de-personalizes the home by removing as much of the owner and their life as possible within the residence.

- Staging removes taste-specific colors and items from the décor, since these are also a reflection of the current owner and therefore are related to the likability of the property in general.

- Staging will provide an improved layout of all interior spaces, including furniture and accessories. This will enhance traffic flow and aggrandize interior space. Rooms will look and feel larger and more functional.

- Staging defines spaces to make it easier for buyers to see their worth. Nothing will be left to the imagination as to the exact purpose of every room. Form and function become one inseparable asset in every room.

To summarize this home staging foundations section, it should now be clear why staging is not simply decorating. Instead, it is real estate marketing. Home staging differs from many other design arts in that it takes into account the psychological and sociological factors which exist in the minds of every real estate buyer, no matter how savvy they might be.

Home Staging History

Property staging has actually been around for a very long time. In fact, as long as people have been selling, renting and trading real estate, there has been some form of aesthetic staging in existence. It makes sense to fix up anything that you intend to sell, since a nicer version of the product will move faster and potentially go for more money. People have been specifically making real estate more appealing in order to create a better sale opportunity for thousands of years.

Currently there are a number of people who consider themselves to be the sole founder or one of the innovators of home staging. This is certainly an egotistical view, since staging has been going on for countless generations. Of course, there are people who helped develop the modern staging profession, but even this career has been around for a long time, although often integrated into associated job titles, such as real estate agent, real estate broker, contractor, interior designer and decorator. I am not going to fuel any fires by giving my own opinion about who is responsible for what when it comes to modern home staging, but I do feel that all involved aggrandize their role more than is just.

Modern property staging has only been around for a historical blink of an eye. What we now deem "home stagers", that is professionals who only deal in preparing properties for rent or sale, is a very new innovation in the real estate industry. The reasons why this profession has exploded with activity are simple. The job performed by staging professionals is extremely valuable. So valuable in fact, that dedicated workers are needed to do it, since staging can offer many tangible and proven benefits to property owners of all types, who are looking to sell their real estate investments.

So now we know that there is a great demand for staging professionals, but it is still interesting to see how the industry evolved from a group of decorators and design insiders to a fully organized, respected and efficient industry unto itself. As for how this happened, once again, it depends on whom you ask. Regardless, it is a natural progression for related industries to gravitate together and develop synergy, and this is exactly what happened to form the property staging universe.

Decorators, furniture rental companies, moving services, contractors and real estate agents all work together anyway and many people in these businesses are involved in multiple facets of the industry at the same time. As more people realized there was a definite advantage to working on improving the look and feel of a home before selling it, criteria were formed to determine the best ways to enhance the property, while still being able to recoup the cost. Input was gathered from all these professions and the results were the cosmic dust which created home staging.

From humble beginnings to a now booming and ever-expanding industry, staging has clearly cut out a niche for itself in the real estate sector. The staging business is expanding at a truly remarkable rate and now is the time to get in, while the getting is good!

History is a "soft science" and when the facts are so new and still being uncovered, many inconsistencies are found. So, for those who claim to be the father, or mother of home staging, good for you. Just go on thinking that you started the shot heard round the world. That's fine. For the rest of you, please know the facts. Staging has been alive and well since mankind has determined that property has a value. Furthermore, that this value can be increased by making the property more appealing. Therefore it comes down to math...

- **Property Value** is directly related to **Desirability**
- **PV** conditional to **D**
- Improving **Property** increases **Desirability**
- **+P =+D**
- **Therefore, +D =+PV**

Conclusion, a more desirable property is worth more money. Modern statistics support this statement 100%, but go on to tell us even more about the relationship between home staging and property value.

Home Staging Statistics

Home staging has been studied exhaustively by insider and independent research groups of all types. The real estate industry has spent large sums of money and invested considerable effort into determining the parameters in which home staging should be used, as well as defining how much staging cost is "too much" or "too little" to justify the return on investment. This is all very complicated for novices to comprehend. But, it is crucial to understand and appreciate the conclusions drawn from these years of past research, as well as the ongoing efforts being utilized to continually guide the staging industry to full development. So, without further adieu, here are some of the proven conclusions from a battery of statistical studies:

Staged Homes Sell Faster

Typically, staged homes sell 2 to 2.5 times faster than comparable unstaged properties in identical real estate market conditions, regardless of the strength or condition of the market.

Staged Homes Sell for More Money

Staged properties sell for up to 17% higher than comparable unstaged properties in an identical real estate market, regardless of the relative strength of that market.

Home Staging is an Excellent Investment

Staging is one of the best dollar-for-dollar investments you can possibly make in your home, prior to sale.

These are the statistics provided by the experts. As a working staging consultant in New York, I can comment on my own personal experience with real estate in the metropolitan area, as well as the suburban areas where I live. In my market, I notice staged homes do sell statistically accurate at 2 to 2.5 times faster. I have seen this occur in the best real estate markets (such as 2005) and the worst, (such as 2009).

As far as extra profitability, I can say that real estate in New York is already very expensive, but staging raises the asking price and final price an average of 5% to 15% from my own statistics. So, let's discuss what this means for you, as a homeowner or aspiring home stager.

In New York City, real estate is at a premium. Maintaining real estate is also very expensive and ongoing monthly expenses can break anyone's bank account. Selling a home faster is always better, since it allows the seller freedom to move definitively on to their own new property aspirations. Additionally, it allows sellers to cut the financial ties and attachments of their old home sooner, eliminating the need to pay ongoing taxes, mortgages, utilities, maintenance and other associated fees.

As far as extra income earned through the staging process, let's look at 4 examples of saleable properties here in New York. Yes,

these do represent the average client I have in my area
profits are actual numbers pulled from my files and ar
representative of my business as a whole. The price fo
your area is likely to differ, but the percentage of increased
profitability using home staging is likely to remain the same.
(Unstaged actual value determined by real estate agent based on
years of regional experience, current listing prices and
comparable sales.)

- **Unstaged Actual Value** $200,000
- **Post Staging Asking Price** $220,000
- **Sale Price** $210,000
- **Staging Cost** $900
- **Extra Profit** $9,100

- **Unstaged Actual Value** $400,000
- **Post Staging Asking Price** $420,000
- **Sale Price** $422,000
- **Staging Cost** $3,000
- **Extra Profit** $19,000

- nstaged Actual Value $650,000
- Post Staging Asking Price $709,000
- Sale Price $699,000
- Staging Cost $5000
- Extra Profit $44,000

- Unstaged Actual Value $1.2 million
- Post Staging Asking Price $1.4 million
- Sale Price $1.4 million
- Staging Cost $15,000
- Extra Profit $185,000

Please take a good look at these statistics and ask yourself if you could use that extra profit as a result of your home sale. Do you think that you could convince real estate sellers that you can make them more money by hiring you to perform home staging? Are you ready to read more?

Staging Your Home for Sale

Ok, so now you are interested in receiving the many benefits of home staging for yourself. Maybe you are thinking of starting a career in home staging and need to begin learning how to do it.

Let's get started! In order to maximize the beneficial aspects of real estate staging, it is crucial to stage the home fully, before listing the property for sale. This is so important; I will say it again...

<u>STAGE</u> THE HOME AND THEN <u>LIST</u> THE HOME

The reason why it is so important to stage <u>first</u> is that the staging design will provide the following additional benefits during the listing process:

- **Staging will drive up the list price decided upon by the real estate agent.**

- **Staging will facilitate incredible MLS and advertising photos.**

- **Staging will welcome the first visitors to the property, who are likely to be real estate agents. Once the word is out about how terrific the property looks, a sale will not take long.**

Once you have decided that you will actually sell any piece of real estate, or help a seller to fulfill their marketing of a property, this is the time to begin working on a staging plan. Remember that some of the strategies involved in staging may take some time, so it is best to begin immediately and leave yourself time to complete all aspects of the process. For a moment, let's focus on people who are looking to learn staging to prepare their own homes for sale. For readers who are using this book to learn home staging as a career, put yourself in your prospective client's shoes and think as they will before hiring you. The big decision that you have to make now is:

"HOW DO I WANT TO STAGE MY HOME?"

Professional Staging Versus DIY

Considering whether to hire a professional home stager, perform do-it-yourself property staging or compromise somewhere in between is one of the hardest choices for many home sellers. This is one of the decisions which will eventually determine how well the staging project will work and how much it will cost. While there is no universal answer which will advise homeowners on the best approach for them, there are logical and sensible guidelines which can help you make up your mind as to the ideal staging method for you and your family.

Option 1: Hire a Professional

Hiring a home stager is always an excellent idea. These people are industry professionals and will surely be able to deliver incredible property aesthetics using proven and practiced staging strategies. The upside of hiring a home stager is that the work will be top-notch and the entire project will be done with little or no effort from the homeowner. The downside of professional home staging includes a higher cost than other forms of staging and possible liability issues with furniture and art rental for families with young children and pets. Remember that professionals likely to bring in new décor items and these furnishings are your responsibility while they remain in your home. Young kids and pets might cause damage to these rented items, necessitating repair or replacement at your expense.

Option 2: DIY

DIY or do-it-yourself home staging is a good option for sellers who do not mind investing sweat-equity in order to save money. DIY is very popular throughout the home improvement industry and preparing a property for sale is another opportunity to get your hands dirty and hold on to more of that hard-earned cash. The advantage to DIY is obvious: It is the cheapest way to stage a home. The disadvantage is that is can be quite a bit of work and the design end may be prohibitively confusing or even impossible for novices to figure out. Remember, making improvements in your home's décor is great, but you have to know which changes to make!

Option 3: Hiring a Consultant

Home staging consultants, such as myself, offer a fantastic compromise for families who fall in the middle of these 2 options. Many people like the idea of saving money using DIY staging, but are just not sure how to begin or what exactly to do. Hiring a consultant will provide you with a home staging expert, who will design the entire staging project for you, but allow you to actually do the work yourself to save the majority of the cost compared to full service real estate staging. The advantages of this approach include a low price tag, typically only a few hundred dollars more than complete DIY staging, as well as the benefit of a blueprint detailing exactly what needs to be done to stage the home and how to do it. The downside of using a staging consultant is a slightly increased cost over DIY and the fact that you still have to execute the design on your own. Personally, I found this to be the best approach for many average families who are selling their homes, since it offers the best of both worlds. This is precisely why I set up my business to follow the consultant model.

Choosing a Staging Method

Here is a quick synopsis of your home staging options:

Staging Option	Advantages	Disadvantages
Professional Stager	* Everything done for you * Excellent results	* Higher cost * Rental issues
DIY	* Lowest cost * No rental liabilities	* You must do everything * Design is difficult
Staging Consultant	* Design Aspect covered * Excellent compromise	* You still have to execute the design

Obviously, if you are good with your hands and have solid design and decorating skills, the DIY approach suits you perfectly. If you do not have the time, energy, skills or knowledge to perform the physical or artistic aspects of DIY, then hiring a professional stager is ideal. If you want to save money and are not sure you can handle designing a staging plan, but are confident that you can follow detailed instructions, then hiring a staging consultant is best for you.

Personally, I recommend full service professional staging for very busy people and people who do not have any DIY skills at all. Additionally, full service is well suited for families without young children or pets, since there is no liability with rented or loaned furniture, art or accessories. Finally, I virtually always recommend professional full service staging for high-end, luxury properties.

In my experience, the "average" family selling a home is often best served by hiring a staging consultant. This option allows them to have expert design and guidance on the planning end and full freedom to implement the design in the ways which work best for their needs. I am thrilled to say that I work with "average" home sellers all the time as my primary business model.

For those sellers who are interested in DIY home staging, there is a wealth of informative resources, including this book, to help you accomplish all your aesthetic property improvement goals. There have been many books and magazine articles written about home staging, both in print and on the internet. Additionally, many television shows feature segments on real estate staging and some shows are completely dedicated to the staging industry. Channels such as HGTV and The DIY Network are chock-full of quality programming which is sure to be a real asset to anyone considering a property staging project.

Time and Cost of Home Staging

The 2 common questions I get about home staging are:

How long will it take?

and

How much will it cost?

Unfortunately, there are no definitive answers for either of these inquiries, since there are many variables used to provide parameters for the correct reply.

As far as time goes, it all depends on how well versed the stager is at what they do. Professionals can have furniture, art and accessories delivered and the entire design complete within a few days time. This makes professional staging perfect for time-crunched sellers. DIY will usually take longer, but not necessarily.

I always advise sellers to begin the organizational and furnishing removal phases of staging long before the decorating part. This way, much of the work is accomplished, a little at a time, so as to not pressure the homeowner too much. Hiring a staging consultant will speed up the DIY process, since the pro will be able to design an expert plan within a day or two and then the seller simply has to follow the directions to get it all done.

The cost of home staging is another huge variable. Many sources suggest spending 1% to 2% of the total asking price of the home, but I think these guidelines are a bit high in many instances, but just right in other situations. The main reason for my wavering of whether this is an appropriate cost estimate is the price of the home. I feel that $1000 might be a fair budget for a $100,000 condo, but I do not think that a 30 million dollar house will typically require $300,000 of staging fees.

So, let's talk in relative terms: Professional staging is the most costly option and ongoing rental fees for furniture and art (if applicable) will make the cost rise as the home stays on the market longer. Staging will help the home to sell faster, but it still might linger if the housing market is truly abysmal, the price is simply too high or if the home has serious issues unrelated to the staging. These factors can make professional staging with continuing fees open-ended for total cost. This is an idea that scares me and many potential clients. This is why many stagers and furniture rental companies greatly discount the month-to-month fees based on continuing need for furnishings to remain in place within the home. In fact, renting furniture for a year might only cost 3 times the cost of renting it for a month. In most cases, this solves any concerns a client may have with the possibility of prohibitive ongoing costs.

The cost of DIY staging is far lower and really only covers the items which need to be bought or rented independently. Typically this cost is as little as $100 and usually maxes out at about half the cost of professional home staging, depending on the extent of work which is required. I staged my own smaller-than-average sized home for $400. This project made me back $35,000 in added profit. Most DIY stagers can enhance an average house or apartment with lots of sweat-equity and a total cost of $500 to $2000.

The cost of using a staging consultant is about the same as DIY staging, plus the fees charged by the staging professional for their consulting service. In my experience, this is usually about $200 to $700, on top of the DIY costs. However, these fees save huge amounts of time and prevent wasting money on ill-conceived and amateurish staging ideas common to the pure DIY approach. Total cost, on average $700 to $2500.

Remember that the cost of living in your particular geographic area will affect these numbers greatly. I live and work in New York City and Long Island, which are very costly places to do anything. You will certainly get more for your money in many other areas of the country and the world.

SECTION 2:

Interior Home Staging Basics

Furniture Rental vs. Existing Décor

Before we get into the actual staging strategies which will work to improve the aesthetics of a home, let's talk for a minute about the idea of using existing décor items versus renting new items for your staging plan. Professional home stagers often lean towards the idea of renting furnishings and sometimes may insist upon it. DIY stagers typically lean towards keeping as much of their current décor as possible, often in an attempt to save some money. There are advantages and disadvantages on both sides of the equation.

Renting generally works better to optimize the room décor. However, this is not always true, especially in cases where the current décor is well designed and charming. Renting furniture will allow a seller to easily change the style of the home, updating the interior for little money, which can be a huge asset for outdated and worn properties. However, renting also may entail a delivery fee for furniture and will likely also mean paying ongoing rental fees month by month, until to the home is sold. Finally, renting may not be a good idea for families with young children and pets, since these little guys can cause big damage to potentially expensive leased furniture and art, costing lots of money for repair or replacement.

Using the existing décor is nice, since the cost is low or free. It is also faster and more flexible in scheduling than utilizing rental items. However, the results are likely to be limited and will be greatly dependent on the quality and appeal of the present décor. Of course, there are many ways to spruce up the current furniture, using paint, new hardware and slip covers. Dated or ill-maintained furniture can be enhanced quickly and easily with a coat or two of white or black paint. New hardware can make an old bedroom set or desk look brand new. Slipcovers and new throw pillows can neutralize and improve worn or taste-specific couches, chairs and other fabric covered items. Obviously, these repairs are low cost and mostly consist of sweat equity methods, making them the ideal complement for do-it-yourself staging or tightly-budgeted professional interventions.

Declutter the Home

One of the first things you need to do is declutter. I rarely see a home which is not incredibly cluttered. You need to remove all these distractions, so that buyers can concentrate on the home itself, not the stuff contained therein.

Decluttering is easy. Basically, just pack up all the furnishings which will not be part of the staging design and place them in storage. Remove alternate seasonal clothing from the closets and store them, as well. Pack up all collections, knick knacks and excess everything, and store it! Do not pack this stuff away into the basement, attic or closets, unless you happen to have a vast storage space in the garage, attic or basement and can arrange these items neatly. It is a better bet to rent a storage unit and pack up these items up in preparation for the impending move. This will save time later, as well.

- **<u>Helpful Hint:</u>** This should be the first thing you do in your staging project!

- **<u>Helpful Hint:</u>** If it is not an absolute necessity, place it in storage.

<u>Depersonalize the Home</u>

It is also crucial to depersonalize the interior space. This means removing the current occupant's style from the home. Take down and pack up all those collections. Take down and pack up all those dusty photos. I know they are sentimental, but they are not meaningful to prospective buyers. Remove any item which is atypical for a home to contain, such as an improvised putting range, huge craft area (taking over the kitchen table), scrapbooking room (instead of dedicated guest quarters) or a shrine to an all-time favorite rock band. All these things are incredibly distracting to buyers and will throw them off course when they are viewing the property.

There is nothing wrong with the occupant's taste, décor, style, furniture, accessories, palate of colors and everything thing else which makes the house a home. These things are all a part of the person's life and they can take them anywhere they move in the world.

However, if the seller actually wants to move, then they might have to compromise their own unique style for a short time to make the home more appealing to an "average buyer". This is where home staging comes into play. Prospective buyers do not want to buy the current occupants life. They want to purchase a piece of their own paradise.

- **Helpful Hint:** You want to be remembered as the lovely home with the fine décor, not the home with the huge Elvis Presley wall of memorabilia... Enough said.

Neutralize the Décor

It is important to neutralize the décor of the home and remove taste-specific items, colors and furnishings. You do not want buyers reflecting on and judging the present taste and style, be it boring, eclectic, exotic or kitschy. You want them to see a nice neutral palate of colors and furnishings which reflects the idyllic lifestyle they want to have if they purchase the home.

How do you know if something is taste-specific? This can be tricky. You need to get some knowledgeable opinions from someone who knows until you gain an experienced eye to make objective judgments. If you are using DIY staging, you can ask your friends and family, but they are likely to provide lip service to your exquisite taste in decorating. It is better to be objective yourself or ask your real estate agent. The best choice would be to ask a professional home stager or hire a staging consultant. They will certainly get your home sorted quickly and efficiently!

If you are an aspiring stager, you must cultivate an eye for what sells and what does not sell. Take time to pursue all avenues of learning and peer networking to develop your skills. It takes an investment of time and effort to become good at anything and home staging is no exception. I provide many location-specific strategies on what should be done and what should be avoided throughout my website. Be sure to refer to this resource often as part of your continuing educational process.

- **<u>Helpful Hint:</u>** Do not go with a "themed" design, unless it is appropriate to the home's situation. For example, neutralize a tropical-themed home, unless the home actually is located in the tropics!

- **<u>Helpful Hint:</u>** Do not attempt to impress buyers with visual tales of the occupant's life and travels. An international décor is wonderful, but just keep it reasonable and appealing. No animal heads from hunting, mounted trophy fish or stuffed deceased pets.

<u>Staging Furniture</u>

Furniture is the main ingredient in interior decorating. Furniture for your use must suit the needs and preferences of your family in functionality, budget and design. However, these ideas are not important when considering furniture for home staging purposes. The most important consideration when staging a home for sale is choosing furniture which will help create that concept of <u>universal appeal</u> that we spoke of earlier.

Furniture items should maintain a cohesive design throughout the home. Do not mix and match styles, as this will give a disjointed and scattered appearance. Choosing the style of furniture will depend greatly on the type of home in which it will be placed and the target buyer demographic. For example, if you are actively trying to sell to retirees and empty-nesters, a traditional furniture style might be the best choice. If you were staging a totally renovated loft in a trendy futuristic building, modern style would be appropriate. If you are not sure what style to chose, I generally recommend contemporary, since this look and feel will update the home, make it warm and welcoming and also suit the tastes of most buyers.

Selecting furniture items and placement should be accomplished using proportion as a main criterion. It is vital to choose furnishings which fit the space well and look right in the room. Choosing furniture which is too small will waste the openness of a large space, making the furniture look odd and dwarfed. Choosing furniture which is too large (a very common mistake) will cramp the design and make the room too busy and cluttered. Additionally, it is crucial to place the right amount of furniture in the room. Make sure every piece has a distinctive purpose. Most homes have far too much furniture, so I typically advise removing pieces, rather than adding.

Try to maintain open space around furniture groupings, with traffic flow space of not less than 3 feet wide as a minimum. This will truly make a huge difference in the overall look of the rooms. Do not place furniture in front of scenic views, unless it is low seating designed to take advantage of the vistas. Do not place furniture in traffic flow areas, as this will certainly throw off buyers as they attempt to navigate a path around the home.

- **Helpful Hint:** Moving large and heavy furniture is much easier with furniture gliders. These plastic discs make it possible for 1 person to easily move a large item alone, without damaging floors. They are cheap and can be found at most home stores. Absolutely essential.

- **Helpful Hint:** Today's slipcovers are incredibly attractive and really can not even be detected. Clients will want to keep these on your furniture even after they move. They are a fast fix for old, dated or worn out furniture items.

- **Helpful Hint:** Experiment with placement. If it helps, use 2D modeling to arrange furniture in a simulation without moving a thing. Simply use graph paper to represent the room and cut out colored cardboard to represent furniture. Assign a consistent scale for accurate results, say 1 square=1 foot of actual space. This will allow you to view all possible layouts fast and easily, without any back-breaking labor.

Staging with Art

Art and accessories can really do a tremendous amount to enrich the décor of any home. This is why many stagers will choose to use art over furniture to define the look and feel of many rooms. Art should reflect the style of the home and the general décor, but can push the boundaries slightly in order to really stand out. This is especially true for art which is being staged as a focal point of a room.

Do not choose art which may be offensive or controversial, since these aspects may be counterproductive to your goal of achieving universal appeal. Do choose art with emotional messages, as long as they are positive and reflective of the environment.

Art can be purchased, rented or made. Personally, I think all three options work well for most staged properties. Most people have some lovely art, although they may not be using it wisely or at all. I often find wonderful unused items in people's attics and garages. DIY art can be made out of virtually anything, with most projects costing only a few dollars and producing fantastic results. Purchasing art is fine, if the client intends to take it with them and will enjoy it in their new home. If not, art rental is a great option which will allow the stager to furnish the home with the latest creations from popular masters. Art rental comes with the same cautions for damage as furniture rental, so use care in making your decision.

Art includes paintings, sculpture, photography, improvised and salvaged items, metal work, natural materials and many other forms. It is nice to mix and match different types of art, when feasible, for a steady flow of interest in the design. Make sure to display art prominently or do not bother at all. Art should be seen as part of the décor, not separate, so be sure to integrate it into the overall design sense of the room.

- **Helpful Hint:** Hang wall mounted art in the best space for your design intention. If the art is to be seen and enjoyed, hang it at eye level. Most people hang art too high. If the art is being used to draw the eye upwards to play-up a desirable architectural feature, such as a high, tray or domed ceiling, or exquisite crown molding, be sure to hang it in a vertical grouping, leading the eye up towards the intended destination naturally and effortlessly.

- **<u>Helpful Hint:</u>** Art can often be used to fill problem areas of the home where furniture just does not work. Art can provide a necessary design element in tight spaces, traffic flow areas and awkward spaces for a balanced aesthetic.

<u>Staging with Proportion</u>

Proper proportion is critical to any good property staging design. It is necessary to choose furniture and accessories which reflect the size and scope of the space. For example, rooms with tall ceilings benefit from art and accessories which reach upwards to draw attention to the expansive ceiling dimensions, while rooms with large square footage benefit from wider and visually heavier furniture. It is rare that people select items which are too small for a space, but it is very common that they choose items which are too large. Furniture which is too big will diminish the perceived size and functionality of a space, making it appear cramped and cluttered. Do not fall into this trap.

Do not forget to include open space in your design, as well. Proportionate amounts of open space must be accounted for in the same manner as defined and occupied space. Do not leave too much open space or the room will look empty, while leaving too little open space will make the room too busy.

- **Helpful Hint:** Breaking the room into sections which are defined by use will assist you in finding proportionate furnishings. For example, a seating grouping sized to the entire room may be too large, while a seating grouping sized to the specific area of the room that it occupies will be just right.

Staging with Open Space

Open space is area which is not occupied with furnishings. Instead, it is the air and breathing room in between the furnishings. Open space is a critical factor in good design. Without its inclusion, one furnishing blends into the next, with a heavy, busy and cluttered feeling.

Open space provides visual and actual comfort, enabling people to move about the home better and provides more personal space to each occupant of a room. Additionally, open space also helps to separate and define grouped furnishings, providing obvious functionality to each sector of space.

In order to utilize open space in a staging design, keep looking at the room from different angles. If items seem to blend together too much, there is likely to be too little open space. If items look distant and isolated from one another, there is likely to be too much. Keep open space and furnished space proportionate to each other, depending on the design you are trying to achieve.

- **Helpful Hint:** Open space is not emptiness. It is actually a part of the design, using the principles of texture and color contrast to build an aesthetic décor in the room. Do not look at it as a lack of, but instead look at it as an addition.

Staging with Color

Color is a primary component of interior design. Choosing a color palate can be a daunting task when you are decorating a home for your own use. However, it is far easier when staging a home for sale. Staging theory preaches that in order to achieve universal appeal, the palate of colors should be generally warm and inviting, but still leaning heavily towards neutrals of all shades and especially light earth tones.

Paint is an easy fix for any room and is a perfect DIY project. Let this be the start of your color palate selection. Once the base color of the room is done, be sure to highlight it by painting trim and moldings a contrasting color. I usually recommend bright white for this use.

Furniture can be contrasting in some instances, but coordinating is typically a better option. Art and accessories should be a blend of coordinating and contrasting tones to provide interest and texture. I like to use many shades of the same base color to give a multi-faceted look and feel to a room, even when the color palate is rather narrow.

taste neutral

Taste specific colors must go. There is no way around it. Bright or dark paint jobs and furnishings in horrific colors will have buyers running for the door. Do not allow the colors of a room to dictate the saleability of the property. Do not be offended by the suggestion to paint and do not offend your clients. It is not a reflection on their taste, but instead, just another of the many strategies involved in comprehensive real estate marketing.

- **Helpful Hint:** Do not paint white on the walls, except in very rare instances. Rather, use some color, even if it is a basic off-white or earth-tone shade. Multiple shades of the same base color work to liven up homes and provide added detail and texture.

- **Helpful Hint:** Painting is cheap and easy. This will allow you to take chances with your design. If you do not like the results, you can always paint over them. Nothing ventured, nothing gained.

- **Helpful Hint:** Accent walls are a fast and inexpensive design element which can dress up any room and help define individual spaces. They are particularly effective in large rooms and open concept floor plans.

Home Staging Floors

Floors are always an important part of the interior décor of any home. Currently, hardwood floors have enjoyed a tremendous boost in popularity and homeowners who are lucky enough to have them are reaping the benefits to their home's value. Other flooring options include laminate flooring, tile, slate, bamboo, concrete and carpet, among others.

Flooring should always be inspected for condition and cleanliness before placing a home on the market. Here are some specific tips regarding the various types of flooring likely to exist in your home:

Hardwood flooring should be exposed if available and in good condition. Carpeting may have protected your floors and they may not even require refinishing. I was lucky enough to find beautiful 85 year old original oak flooring in my English Tudor, which had been protected for years by thick shag carpeting. Needless to say, the flooring has become a major asset to my home. If your floors do require sanding and refinishing, take on the project. Do it yourself or hire a pro. Either way, you are likely to see a tremendous return on your investment.
Never hide hardwoods.

Laminate flooring is better quality and easier to install than ever before. Laminates can be laid over virtually any surface and are a quick, easy and inexpensive fix for almost any flooring concern. Laminates are a nice budget-friendly option to achieve the look of hardwood at a fraction of the cost. Laminates come in a vast selection of colors, patterns and styles to suit any décor and application throughout your home.

Tile floors are popular in the kitchen, bath and house-wide in warm, tropical locales. Tiles are easy to install and can be very cheap, with labor as the main consideration. If you can install tile yourself, you can re-do huge areas of your home for a tiny investment. Ceramic is the most cost effective option, while marble, porcelain and granite are pricier.

Slate flooring is one of my personal favorites, but can be too taste-specific for some buyers. This is an option which may be substituted for tile and can truly present a high-end finish to any room. The best part about slate is that it is a breeze to install.

Bamboo flooring is an alternative to wood or laminate and is especially suited for an eco-friendly design. Bamboo is likely to become more and more popular over the next few years and I anticipate costs to come down significantly, making it one of my recommended materials for any room.

Carpet is always an option, but is generally not a buyer-pleaser. If you have carpet, make sure it is stain-free and not overly worn. If it is in poor condition, replace it or better yet, install another material for greater appeal. Do not keep old, ugly or dated carpeting. This will create a huge liability for the value of your home. Instead, invest in new carpeting, or better yet, laminate flooring, for a fresh clean look and feel.

- **Helpful Hint:** Laminate flooring gets the nod for the most versatile and inexpensive option for floors which need some serious help. It can be installed anywhere, looks fantastic and is easy to maintain. Best of all, it is an ideal DIY project.

- **Helpful Hint:** Hardwoods can sometimes be brought back to life easily without refinishing. Often, the floor simply needs a new coat of polyurethane or possibly a coat of polyurethane with a built-in stain. I used this approach on my own floors and achieved an amazing effect. They look better than new!

- **Helpful Hint:** Flooring should also be cohesive. Many homes have lovely flooring room to room, but the difference in styles and materials provides a disjointed look and is a bitter disappointment to buyers. Keep colors and materials consistent room to room for a better overall presentation.

Staging with Rugs

Throw rugs and area rugs are always a nice design touch, especially when used to offset a furniture grouping placed on top. Rugs can be very costly, especially for authentic oriental and

Persian designs. However, there are many super cheap and lovely styles available for virtually no monetary investment whatsoever. I have bought some truly designer-quality rugs for as little as $30!

Rugs will soften the look and feel of any room with a hard flooring surface, providing extra comfort for the feet and eyes. Rugs are a great way to disperse color at the lowest level of the room and can also be crucial in achieving aesthetic balance of décor components. I am a big fan of rugs for home staging designs, as well as day-to-day use. I have one in almost every room in my own home.

When placing rugs, do not float them in the room, unless the space is a foyer or other open area. Many people like to place them in front of furniture groupings, but this is a design faux pas in most cases. It is better to anchor the rug to the furniture by insuring that at least the front legs of the furniture are on the rug, creating a cohesive grouping. This can be a bit of a burden if the furniture is already placed, so be sure to position the rug first, then place the furniture on top.

- **Helpful Hint:** I like discount home stores for rugs. There are some great rugs at Home Depot, but I believe IKEA and Wal-Mart (online) to be the overall best values for most contemporary designs.

- **Helpful Hint:** Rugs can act almost like art. I like to use contemporary rugs to update more traditional furniture styles and breathe new life into a stuffy space. Rugs are also a great way to add punches of color. Beautiful rugs can make excellent wall hangings, for super economical large art installations.

Home Staging Lighting

Lighting is always a very important part of the décor to consider when staging your home. One of the most common complaints that most buyers have about the properties they view is that the home is too dark. Make sure that your lovely home does not fall into this category, since a dismal environment is likely to be passed over, regardless of how nice everything else may be inside.

Illumination consists of both natural light and artificial light. Optimizing natural light is easy with the right window treatments, but artificial light can be more complicated. I recommend that you install a variety of lighting options in every room and experiment to see how each can be used to suit the specific design requirements of the space. Overhead lighting is traditional in most homes and is usually hardwired. Table and floor lamps are easy to place almost anywhere and provide either direct or indirect lighting to the space. Upward facing lighting projects illumination towards the ceiling and is a key component of mood lighting and atmosphere enhancement.

Many lighting fixtures and lamps can also serve an artistic design function, as well. A beautiful fixture can be substituted for a sculpture or accessory and is viewed as both aesthetically pleasing and functional, making it a real winner.

When showing your home, be sure to turn on all the lights, since this will insure a positive impression and chase away the "too dark" comments before they can occur. Place as many lighting sources as possible on dimmers, to truly control the intensity and effect of the illumination. This is the ideal solution for areas which suffer hot spots and dark spots. Simply place more fixtures throughout the room and use the dimmers to brighten or lessen each fixture's overall contribution to the atmosphere.

— Staging minute video
— styps in process
videos—

Lighting is also a major consideration outside the home. Hard-wired lights, such as on the porch and driveway, should always be turned on when showing the home in the afternoon and evening. Consider attaching motion detectors to conserve energy and increase security from these lighting sources.

Do not forget to add other sources of external light to the yard and front of your home. Colored spot lights look wonderful on architectural features and landscaping focal points. Outdoor fixtures, and even rope lighting, can provide a festive environment for the backyard. Large yards should feature illumination facing away from the main home, as well. This will define the size of the yard and provide added useable space any time of day or night.

- **Helpful Hint:** Lighting is inexpensive and can make a huge difference inside or outside the home. Best of all, most lighting sources can be taken with you when you move, making the investment a really palatable expenditure.

- **Helpful Hint:** Installing new fixtures is a great way to really change the interior of your home for the better. Plan the lighting you will need and then buy your own fixtures for best value. Bring in a qualified electrician to install, unless you are capable of doing it yourself. The most positive effects will be seen in the kitchen, bathroom and dining room, where old fixtures really have a negative impact on the space.

Home Staging Closets

Staging closets is often one of the universal aspects of a property enhancement project throughout the residence. Closets are always an important part of a home and figure into a buyer's wish-list tremendously. Having large closets is an asset, but even the largest closets need to be arranged properly to show off their storage potential. Likewise, smaller closets can be optimized to appear bigger and more functional through careful staging strategies.

½ Stuff + matchng hangers plz

First, clean out all the closets in the home and pack up all the unfrequently used items and seasonal possessions and clothing. Getting these packed now and sent to storage will provide a head start for the impending move. Do not give in to the urge to remove clutter from the room and place it in the closet. This will defeat all your hard work. You want to avoid clutter completely, not transfer it somewhere else.

Large closets should be organized with lots of shelves, covered storage options and clothing bars. Small closets can benefit from double hanging clothing bars for 2 levels of storage or placing enclosed storage containers in the floor of the closet. Good storage options are wood or wire racks with opaque drawers or baskets to provide a neat look and privacy for your personal possessions. Do not use cardboard boxes or those plastic pull-out drawers or bins. These look like junk and will make your closet look horrific.

Try to keep your closet filled to about one third of its total capacity. While this might sound difficult, it will make a huge difference in the perceived size of the space. Rotate clothes out more often to accomplish this goal. Using wooden hangers will also make the space nicer, more aesthetic and more organized.

Professional closet organizing systems can be a real asset, but must be installed properly to benefit the space. Double check all clothing hanging bars and shelves to be sure they are secure and properly installed. If space allows it, consider adding a shoe rack or other specialized storage option, especially in walk-in closets.

- **Helpful Hint:** Reconfiguring the storage options and clothing hanging bars in a typical closet can add up to 80% more useable space, especially in older construction homes.

- **Helpful Hint:** Double check that closet doors work properly, close completely and do not squeak. These are all simple fixes, but are details that buyers will notice. Do not let seemingly insignificant annoyances ruin your hard work.

remove ripped screens

Staging Windows

Staging windows is easy and rewarding, since the windows in your home provide natural light, aesthetic enhancement and scenic vistas. While it is impossible to make your windows larger without costly and time-consuming renovation, it is rather simple to make your windows appear bigger, fuller and more functional using a few focused staging techniques.

Let's begin with the windows themselves. First off, they should be thoroughly cleaned inside and out, as well as inspected for proper hardware operation. It is better to show off windows by removing the screens, whenever possible, since this allows a better view of outside. This is especially crucial for scenic windows overlooking valuable natural landscape features.

Window treatments are one of the aspects of interior design that most people get wrong when staging their homes. Always remove heavy, old curtains and draperies, as well as any type of plastic miniblinds, dated vertical blinds or improvised "bedsheet on the window" ideas. Instead, invest in some inexpensive light and airy window treatments, such as wood blinds, cellular shades, airy curtains, sheer panels, bamboo shades, shoji screens or interior shutters. Most of these can be found at deep discounts at off-price home stores and are perfect DIY projects.

If you are hanging curtains or panels, leave off any top valence for a contemporary look and place the window treatments ceiling to floor for maximum effect. This will make the windows appear larger, the ceilings taller and will also add an updated look and feel to the room.

Keep the visual path to windows unobstructed, allowing more of the great outdoors to come inside. Avoid placing visually heavy or tall furniture near windows for a more spacious look to the room. The common practice of "framing a window" with 2 tall pieces of furniture should be avoided.

- **Helpful Hint:** Decorative curtain rods and tie backs give a custom look for a tiny price. Always invest in beautiful hanging hardware for an upgraded appearance.

- **Helpful Hint:** Overly ornate fabrics and designs are actually distracting and often taste-specific. Keep the window treatments super simple, much like the general décor of the staging for maximum impact. Less is more.

Staging Doors

Staging all the doors in your home is important, but none is more crucial than the entry door to your residence. This door must be particularly detailed with the very best property staging strategies.

The main door, or entry door, should be staged inside and out for maximum appeal. Outside, be sure that surrounding features, such as the address numbers, mailbox, knocker, doorbell and outdoor lighting are all fresh and coordinated in color, pattern and style. Placing a nice wreath on the door is sometimes a good idea, but do not even think about using anything which contains plastic. Make it natural materials for a high-end look or nothing at all, ok? The front door should be freshly painted in a contrasting color to your home. I like red, hunter green, tudor brown and cottage blue, depending on the type of home and the color scheme in effect. Inside, make sure the doorway area is clean, uncluttered and free of soil and dirt common to most entryways.

Secondary entrance doors should be clean and operate easily with all locking mechanisms working smoothly and squeak-free. Sliding doors, such as out to the yard or patio, should be cleaned particularly well and inspected to be sure they operate effortlessly and close securely.

Check the arrangement of outdoor furnishings on the exterior of the home if they are visible from the sliding doors. Make sure that they create an artistic and desirable space that will draw buyers out to the yard, rather than disappoint with a crowded and messy atmosphere which will have buyers turning around and leaving faster than you would like.

Interior doors in the home should be painted or stained to coordinate with the color palate. Natural wood doors are a very nice touch, so consider stripping old paint and refinishing if this look will complement your décor. Check that all interior doors open and close fully, without getting hung up on carpeting or improperly installed framing. Inspect locks on bathrooms and bedrooms to be sure they are functional. Also, double check that doors will not bang into walls or eaved ceilings when buyers come to view the home. If they do make contact, install door stops or other devices to prevent damage to the contact surfaces.

- **Helpful Hint:** Remove large hooks and other bulky hanging devices on the backs of interior doors to allow the door to open completely flush against the wall for a larger look and feel.

- **Helpful Hint:** Don't forget to check closet doors for ease of operation, full closure and squeak-free mechanisms.

- **Helpful Hint:** New door knobs can make a huge difference in the look of your home. Consider replacing old and worn knobs with fresh new styles for superb detailing which buyers will love!

Staging with Moldings

Moldings are one of my favorite items to add to a home's décor for an instant and inexpensive upgrade. Moldings are easy to cut and install and do not require many tools. All you need is a miter saw, brad nailer and a measuring tape and you are ready to go!

If you do not have these tools, they can be purchased for a couple hundred dollars or rented for a few dollars a day.

If you already have nice moldings in your home, be sure to maximize their appeal by painting them with a fresh coat of contrasting paint. I generally recommend bright white for molding applications. Make sure all sections fit the wall well and are securely fastened. If you do not have the luxury of fine moldings, consider adding them to some or all of the rooms in your home for an upgraded appearance.

Moldings can be placed on the baseboard, although most homes already have this feature. Crown moldings are a wonderful way of enriching the ceiling and upper wall joint. Moldings can also be used as chair rails, especially in the dining room, study and living room, or can be utilized to box-out raised shapes on any wall for instant architectural detail and texture. Both chair rails and geometric molding designs work particularly well with 2-tone paint schemes.

- **Helpful Hint:** Always fit angled sections first, then straight sections last, for the best fit.

- **Helpful Hint:** Measure twice, cut once.

- **Helpful Hint:** Bright white moldings work well in virtually any décor. Painting moldings unusual colors is usually not advised.

- **Helpful Hint:** Resin and foam-core moldings can be incredibly detailed and beautiful and are a fraction of the cost of wood. No one will ever know the difference.

- **Helpful Hint:** Buy pre-finished moldings for basic jobs. The cost is only a touch higher than unfinished moldings and the time savings will be substantial.

Staging Architectural Details

Architectural details are artistic and structural enhancements which are built into the home. There are countless examples of architectural details, including banisters, railings, decorative stairways, cupolas, tray ceilings, dome ceilings, wall niches, archways, floor registers, mantles, fireplaces, exposed beams or brick and so many more. If you have lovely and unique details built into your home, it is a great idea to highlight these assets using home staging.

It is generally easy to get buyers to take notice of the fine details in you home. You simply have to capture their attention and direct it towards the target detail. This can be achieved through proper placement of furniture and artwork, as well as maintaining a purposeful traffic flow throughout your home to guide buyers where you want them to go naturally. Lots of open space is crucial to set apart details against your furniture design.

- **Helpful Hint:** Using pops of color in the room near architectural details is one of the easiest ways to draw buyers to notice the property features on their own. This is a nice understated approach.

- **Helpful Hint:** Placing grouped art, lighting or accessories in high locations will draw the eye upwards. Using visually heavy furniture will draw the eye down. Use this to highlight built-in architectural features in your room.

- **Helpful Hint:** Sometimes simply putting a dedicated lighting source on an architectural detail is all you need to do to set it apart from the rest of the décor.

Staging Scenic Views

It is always nice to offer scenic vistas from any window in your home or from your outdoor spaces, such as a deck, patio or terrace. If you are lucky enough to enjoy a scenic view from your property, make sure to play it up as much as possible using staging techniques.

To maximize the aesthetic appeal of beautiful views from inside your home, do everything possible to create an open vantage point from the windows. Do not obstruct the view with furniture, window treatments or an awkward traffic flow. Instead, make sure that buyer will pass the exact place to enjoy the view and pause to notice it.

For outdoor spaces, trim back any trees or landscaping features which may obstruct or diminish a scenic view. Place a decorative accessory to attract attention and buyers will look beyond to notice the beautiful vantage point where they currently stand. If you are blessed with lovely sunsets, try to schedule open houses or viewings to take advantage of this lovely time of day. This is particularly valuable for waterfront properties.

- **Helpful Hint:** As mentioned previously, remove window screens to highlight extremely nice views.

- **Helpful Hint:** Place furniture groupings indoors and out to face scenic vistas and allow buyers to sit and contemplate the fantastic scenery the property enjoys.

Staging Small Rooms

When staging a small room, proportion and layout are the most important considerations. Small spaces can be made to feel larger and more useful, if the items placed in the space are sized correctly for the room. Color is one of those misunderstood myths when it comes to small rooms, since most people believe a light color will enlarge the perceived space. Really, the shade of the room is not nearly as important as the number and size of the furniture items placed there.

The number one rule for small spaces is to remove almost everything which is not crucial. In a bedroom, for instance, leave the bed and only one or two other small pieces of furniture. Even if you have to sacrifice some creature comforts for a few weeks, then so be it. A cramped and cluttered small room is a huge iability, while an open and functional room, regardless of size, is an asset.

- **Helpful Hint:** Scale down everything in the room, including furniture, art, accessories. Think minimalistic and contemporary, with art or lighting providing crucial design interest, without taking up valuable square footage.

- **Helpful Hint:** Try to draw the buyers' eyes upwards, if the ceiling is high. Playing up a tall ceiling height will definitely make the room feel more open and airy.

- **Helpful Hint:** Smaller rooms often benefit from increased contrast in the design elements for optimal separation of décor items.

Staging Large Rooms

Large rooms can be equally challenging as smaller interior spaces. Often, people do not take advantage of a large space and only properly decorate parts of it, filing the rest with "random stuff" in order to make the room appear full. This is a huge mistake. When staging a large room, always start from scratch.

Use open space between furniture groupings to balance out the look and feel of the room. Do not group all the visually heavy items in one area, since this will really destroy any semblance of good design. Many large rooms I stage originally had all the main furniture lumped together and very little of aesthetic value anywhere else in the room. Do not fall into this trap. Spread out the décor, placing furniture into useable groupings, each with a specific purpose. Likewise, do not feel you have to fill every part of the room. Openness is what makes a large room feel large.

Blend common elements into the various parts of the room design to tie all the groupings and vignettes into a cohesive aesthetic. Color is fantastic to accomplish this goal and a few splashes of an accent color will provide all the "glue" your design needs to look solid and balanced.

- **Helpful Hint:** Larger rooms do not necessarily need more furnishings. They may also benefit from a very open design but using proportionately bigger and visually heavier furniture and more weighty accessories.

- **Helpful Hint:** Spacious rooms show better when lighting is used to separate and define sections of the room for specific purposes.

66

Staging an Open Floor Plan

Open concept floor plans are all the rage right now and are truly a puzzling dilemma for many DIY home stagers. The large and flowing interior spaces of open concept can and will be a huge asset to the aesthetic appeal to your home, if and when you stage the room to optimize the advantages of an open flow design.

Open floor plan spaces are sometimes called great rooms. This area generally incorporates the kitchen, dining area and living space into one huge space. It is important to define each area for an obvious use, but still maintain the appeal that open concept affords. This can be accomplished by using repetitive elements throughout every part of the room, while preserving the integrity and identity of each space unto itself.

- **Helpful Hint:** Flooring should be consistent throughout an open concept home. Different flooring surfaces in the living and dining areas will not work well.

- **Helpful Hint:** Paint can be used to tie areas together, but it can also be used to provide accent walls and visual frontiers between defined areas within the room.

- **Helpful Hint:** Open concept generally benefits from minimalistic design sense. Definitely do not clutter the space. I recommend placing accessories and art sparingly and for maximum visual effect, place items to be viewed from at least 2 separate areas at a time. Trying to design each area as a room unto itself will only make the space seem busy and complicated. Instead, consider the entire room as a whole when selecting furnishings and accessories.

Home Repairs

extremely important

Repairs can be one of the most vital aspects of the staging process. It is common for many homeowners to allow small problematic issues to creep up in the maintenance of their home, when a repair can be made easily and inexpensively, often by the owner themselves. Making small repairs around your home will provide a far better sale opportunity, since a properly functioning residence seems better maintained, more structurally sound and more financially appealing.

Some buyers are looking for a fixer-upper. However, the vast majority of potential buyers are not looking to inherit the current owner's headaches, should they decide to purchase the home. Most small repairs are not a big deal for a buyer or a seller.

However, given this as fact, why take chances that you will be turned off by the many problematic concerns th see in your home, when you can fix all of these withou effort or fuss. Before even thinking about staging the décor, make sure the home is structurally sound and all systems are fully operational, as designed.

Small repairs do not mean major renovation work. These are tasks which can usually be DIY projects or may require some measure of professional help. Large scale repairs should be discussed with your real estate agent, since some are necessary, while others might be optional and difficult to recoup the cost.

The more you can learn to do on your own, the less money you will have to invest in repair bills. Luckily, there are a vast number of free resources which you can use to learn how to fix virtually anything in your own home. Your local library will have many books on home improvement and the internet is always the ideal place to look. Here are some of the most common small repairs I advise people to make before listing their home for sale:

- Fix leaking faucets and running toilets
- Repair holes in window and door screens
- Patch holes in walls and paint everything
- Replace old and broken lighting fixtures

Patch cracked concrete outside your home

- Repair broken fences in your yard
- Tighten up loose handrails and banisters
- Fix windows which do not open or close properly
- Make sure the doorbell works
- Repair or replace damaged kitchen appliances
- Replace broken kitchen and bathroom tile
- Repair or replace broken garage doors
- Install or replace smoke and carbon monoxide detectors
- Repair any plumbing or heating system issues
- Be sure electrical outlets work and are up to code, particularly in the kitchen and bathrooms

Repairs may be large scale and costly in some instances. In these cases, weigh the benefits against the expense and speak to your real estate agent for advice. Some potentially costly repairs which should always be done include:

- Water infiltration issues
- Cracked foundations
- Sewer line and water main breaks
- Electrical hazards
- Mold problems
- Serious roofing issues

SECTION 3:

Interior Home Staging Advanced Strategies

Room by Room Strategies

Alright, so now that you have a better understanding of the basics of property staging, let's go through the home, room by room. Here, I will detail some specific techniques which are highly effective for particular areas of the home.

Of course there are no absolutes in interior design and circumstances may alter your specific case recommendations. However, these strategies work for the majority of residences and should be at least partially applicable to every house or apartment. Let's begin with some good general interior staging guidelines:

- Remove all wallpaper if possible.
- Remove all decorative borders in any room.
- No taste-specific themed décor or color palates.
- No plastic or "silk" flowers, plants or trees.
- Make sure to clean and dust everywhere and often.
- Try not to cook odorous foods during home viewings.

- Burn scented candles for showings and open houses.
- No vertical blinds, plastic blinds or dusty blinds.
- No collections or family photo galleries on display.
- Try to place pets with family or friends during the sale process. If not possible, try to confine them to a given area. Do not force your potential buyers to deal with your animals, regardless of whether or not they bite.
- Do not allow children to run the household during a sale. Set rules for them to keep common areas clean and their individual spaces organized. Provide incentive by getting them involved with the staging effort and promising them a reward in your new home. If they are helpful, do not forget to fulfill your promises to them.
- Final rule: When in doubt, take it out! Most interior spaces are just far too cluttered to ever look nice.

Entrance Foyer

The entryway to your home is very important, since it sets the mood for the entire interior tour. If first glances disappoint a prospective buyer, you will have to work twice as hard to get them to have a good feeling about the home later on. Do not take chances. Stage the entrance to your home with extreme care and attention to detail. *We need curtains here*

Every home has a different type of entryway. Some open up into a front porch or mud room, while others provide access to the home directly, as part of an open concept floor plan, through a small hallway or via dedicated landing (common to split level homes). Regardless of how the home opens, here are some tips to follow to insure that potential buyers will be pleased with what they see:

- Keep the entrance as lightly decorated as possible to maintain an open look and feel.
- Do not burden guests with a mess of coats and shoes when they first walk in. Place these neatly out of sight, preferably in a covered storage area or closet.
- Make sure to check this area regularly to keep it immaculately clean and soil free.
- Try to place one striking piece of artwork which can be seen immediately upon entry. This will create interest and draw buyers into the home.
- If you have an interior doormat, invest in a mat which looks nice and conveys a high-end feel.
- Add lighting, if necessary, to provide ample illumination when guests first arrive.

- Be sure that the interior of the front door looks as nice as it does on the exterior. Place a fresh coat of paint if needed.

Living Room

In this living room section, I will cover formal living rooms, dens, family rooms and great rooms. The exact recommendations will vary greatly, depending on the specific set-up of your home. Formal living rooms are a nice feature, but may be too limiting, especially if there is no alternative space for casual family time. If you only have one family room, stage it is a neat, but casual atmosphere. If you are lucky enough to have 2 or more family rooms, then stage one as a formal living room and one or more as casual spaces for together time.

Great rooms should combine the design elements of a living space and a dining room. Make sure to choose how to layout this valuable space very carefully. Remember that each area should be aesthetically-tied to the next for a cohesive design, but still be clearly defined unto itself. This can be accomplished with furniture groupings, layout, placement, painting and open space.

It is always advantageous to have common areas on more than one floor of the home, if viable. Formal living areas should always be on the main floor, close to the dining room and kitchen. Informal family space can be on any level, including the basement, upper level or main floor. Here are some of my specific recommendations for living rooms, family rooms and dens:

- Move furniture off the walls for a more intimate atmosphere. Be sure to choose correct proportions for furniture items.
- Old, worn or dated furniture should be replaced with rental items or covered with sleek new slipcovers for an updated look and feel.
- Do not block windows with tall or visually heavy furniture.
- Try to arrange electronics, such as televisions, video game systems and stereos into covered storage areas. Always hide all visible wiring for a finished look. Best case scenario allows for a wall-mounted flat screen TV.
- Define an obvious focal point in the room. A fireplace works well, but if unavailable, furniture, art, a large window or even a staircase or archway can be a focal point.
- No plastic covers on the furniture.
- Keep the color palate warm and neutral, but not pure white. Use color in fabric, such as throw pillows, coordinating accessories and artwork for aesthetic interest.

- Separate like colors using contrasting colors. Example, do not place a brown sofa on a brown wood floor. Instead, add texture by separating the couch from the floor with a light colored area rug.
- Keep formal living rooms formal. No toys and kiddy items.
- No collections, family photo galleries or other distractions should appear in these rooms. Keep the décor simple and meaningful, by using fewer items, but providing greater impact from each piece of art or accessory. If it does not pop in the room, do not use it.
- Highlight architectural details, such as crown moldings and expansive ceilings, using groupings of art placed at various heights (eye level and up).
- Do not clutter the living space. Most family rooms have way too much going on, trying to accommodate every family member. Staging may require a compromise in your needs to get the home sold. You may have to get rid of that comfy, but ugly chair or that cute plastic swing that junior likes to sit in while watching TV.

Dining Room Staging

Dining rooms are easy to stage, since the design always revolves around the table and chairs. Homes typically have a formal lining room, a casual area for eating, a dedicated dining section of a great room or a combination of more than one option available. No matter how your house or apartment is laid out for lining, certain rules always apply.

First off, make sure that the table is placed in the optimal position in the room. The chairs should be easy to access, without crowding anyone into a wall or corner. If the space is small and feels cramped, downsize the furniture to more manageable proportions. Center a beautiful light fixture 30" to 36" over the table and provide other alternate lighting options in the room, as well. I like indirect lighting with dimmers for a soft glow during dinner.

If the room is large, there may be space and need for other furniture, like a china closet or a sideboard. If the room is not large, do not even consider these items for the space. It is far better to keep this room sparse and open for maximum appeal and functionality. Here are some of my personal recommendations for dining areas of all types:

- Paint this room a warm, appetizing color, but still neutral and classy. Chair rails are a nice touch and can be a perfect DIY project. If you do have a chair rail, a two tone paint job will accent the room perfectly. Do not choose contrasting colors, but instead varying shades of coordinating colors, for a subtle and elegant touch.

- The light fixture will be featured in this room, so invest in a good one. This does not have to be an expensive proposition, as many home stores have wonderful exquisite lighting options for under $150.
- Always set the table as if you were expecting guests for a dinner party. Include full place settings, with plates, silverware, glasses, natural centerpiece flowers and even cloth napkins in rings.
- Nothing paper or plastic on the table, including horrific plastic flowers or "silk" centerpieces.
- Soft music is a nice touch in this room.
- Carpet is a real turnoff in a dining room, so consider removing and replacing it with a solid surface, such as laminate flooring, if feasible.
- Do everything possible to maintain an open and unobstructed traffic flow from the kitchen to the dining space.

Kitchen Staging

Staging the kitchen is one of the main priorities of any real estate marketing plan. A beautiful kitchen is the number one asset a house or apartment can possess and no room will do more to sell your property than this "heart of the home". Luckily, staging a kitchen space is actually quite easy and can usually be accomplished by do-it-yourselfers.

Professionally renovating a kitchen is very costly and time consuming. However, if you have the time and the money, a new kitchen is virtually sure to be a safe investment and you will likely see a full dollar-for-dollar return upon sale. If you can not renovate, or do not require a renovation, then here is a plethora of home staging tips and techniques which can transform any kitchen into an idyllic space:

- Make sure all appliances are functional. Complete minor repairs or replace broken units prior to listing the home for sale.
- Appliances can be painted with specialized enamel (including ranges, with heat-resistant enamel or epoxy) Appliances can also be refinished using durable adhesive films in various colors, including stainless steel.
- Cabinets can be sanded and painted for an updated finish. Change out the hardware to a sleek contemporary design to complete the look for virtually no significant investment.

- Countertops can also be primed and painted with acrylic paints and sealed with food-area-safe clear-coat products.

- Tile and laminate flooring is easy to install in any kitchen. Never leave carpeting in a kitchen.

- Clear off countertops, including removing small appliances. You can leave your coffee maker. Store away all others or place them on dedicated appliance carts for a functional new twist.

- Updating a backsplash is fun and easy with glass tile, subway tile or even stainless steel sheeting.

- Clean out the refrigerator, since people will look inside. Do not pack the fridge super full of food and be mindful of accumulated odors.

- Clean the range and oven inside and out.

- Organize cabinets and do not clutter them with too many dishes, glasses or food items. Instead, go shopping more often and keep cabinets half full for the illusion of more space.

- Make sure the faucet is aesthetically-pleasing and not dripping. Repair or replace if needed. Check for leaks under the sink in waterlines. Do not solve these issues with a small plastic container to catch drips.

- Minimize window treatments in the kitchen to maximize natural light. Additionally, add more than one type of artificial lighting in the room. Always get rid of those old fashioned and unaesthetic overhead florescent fixtures.

- Remove any non-kitchen items or areas from the room. No home office spill-over or homework desk set-ups in this room please.

- Always keep this room perfumed with a food scent like fresh baked bread or vanilla. Avoid non-food scents like flowers, unless you are using real fresh flowers.

- Hide a covered garbage can in a cabinet.

- No pot holders, oven mitts or towels hanging on appliances or from cabinet hardware.

- Absolutely no magnets, photos, kid's drawings or anything on the refrigerator.

- Remove old contact paper from inside cabinets and replace if necessary. Better to leave it off and clean the surface.

Bathroom Staging

Staging the bathrooms in your home is perhaps the second most important facet of real estate marketing, bested only by kitchen staging. Bathroom renovation is pricey and grueling to endure, so most prospective buyers prefer to walk into a home with updated and sparkling baths. Luckily, using basic and advanced staging techniques, renovation is rarely needed, except in the most dire of circumstances.

While the master bathroom is the most important, all the baths should be given due care and effort during staging. Wallpaper should virtually always be removed. The rooms should be painted a relaxing light colored neutral shade. All fixtures should be inspected for wear and tear and small repairs should be made to fix any minor, but potentially damaging issues, such as leaking faucets, running toilets, cracked grout or tiles and outdated lighting. Here are some great staging ideas which work well in virtually any bathroom:

- Old bathtubs, sinks and even tile can be painted for a refreshed look and feel. This is possible using specialized epoxy paints which bond permanently to almost any surface.
- Builder's-grade mirrors and medicine cabinets should be replaced with more aesthetic fixtures for low cost, but high impact improvements.
- Always install fresh toilet seats.

- Rugs are nice in front of the tub and sink(s), but never place a rug in front of the toilet or utilize those carpeted toilet lid covers.
- Remove personal possessions from medicine cabinets and vanity tops. Additionally, clean out all toiletries from the shower and bath area and keep in enclosed storage when showing the home.
- Color coordinate fresh towels, curtains and other accessories for a defined spa-like aesthetic.
- Leave shower curtain or door open when possible to maximize the perceived size of the room.
- Be especially vigilant that this room should be brightly lit at all times.
- Redo old and worn caulking around the tub or shower. Never show a home with mildew on the caulking.
- Organize storage or bathroom closet using only a few towels and accessories to maximize available space.
- Keep scented candles burning to insure the room smells as good as it looks.
- Double check the ceiling for watermarks or drywall deterioration. This is an easy fix, but can scare buyers into thinking there is a serious issue with moisture in the room.

Paint over drips

- If you have a large bath, play up the luxury factor. Add a seating area and some thick and lush spa robes with matching slippers. This will have buyers craving the space and anxious to make an offer.
- The number one rule in bathrooms is always keeping them immaculately clean.

Bedroom Staging

Bedrooms are perhaps the easiest spaces to stage in the home, yet are notorious for making poor appearances during buyer showings. Many people simply do not know what a beautiful bedroom is supposed to look like, so they fall back on what they do know, which is usually a mixture of comfort and functionality but little else. A master bedroom is one of the most important rooms in the home and is always a main consideration on buyer wishlists. Take particular care in staging the master bedroom.

The focal point in any bedroom should be the bed (unless you have a large room with more than one focal point, such as a fireplace or huge scenic window). So, let's discuss some home staging tips which will make the bedrooms stand out from the crowd:

- Remove most of the furniture in the room. Most bedrooms simply have too much going on. A bed is the only thing which must return to the space once staged. All other furnishings should be chosen based on the size and layout of the room. Furnish the space sparsely and do not overdo it with big and heavy furniture, unless the space is huge.
- Choose nice neutral linens and keep the bed made beautifully all the time. Include throw pillows for accents of color.
- Remove all personal items and photos from nightstands and dresser tops. Declutter and depersonalize the space to make it look like a high-end hotel room.
- Use lighting in a variety of ways to add lots of illumination to the room. Do not rely exclusively on overhead lighting. *lamps*
- Keep the window treatments light to optimize natural light from the outside.
- Do not stage an office area in a bedroom. This will make your home look too small and dysfunctional, regardless of its actual size. The only exception is in a 1 bedroom apartment with a large bedroom.
- Include a separate seating or reading area in larger rooms as a nice relaxing "getaway".

- Do not forget to use art in the bedroom. Framed diplomas and other personal memorabilia do not qualify as art.
- Maintain space for traffic flow in the room. Tight spaces and narrow areas will diminish the saleability of the room, so keep open space between furniture items, especially around the bed.
- For an added positive touch, remove telephones and alarm clocks when showing the home. This subtle touch has been shown to make a room appear more relaxing and inviting.
- Don't forget to keep this room scented with nice candles or other high-end atmospheric enhancing product.

Home Office Staging

With more and more people working from home or telecommuting, a home office has fast become one of the assets which can help facilitate a fast and profitable sale. In the past, sellers were always advised to maximize available bedrooms, but now, in many geographic locations and for many target buyer demographics, a home office is a better use of space, especially for smaller, less functional bedrooms.

Never combine a home office into another defined room space. This will make the residence look too small for the buyer's needs and will make buyers look elsewhere for a larger and more functional space. Staging a dedicated home office is fantastic in most markets and is one of the easiest and cheapest rooms to prepare for sale. Here are some of my favorite staging strategies for home office layouts:

- Center the room around the desk. If possible, place the desk in an area with a scenic outdoor view.
- Make sure all the storage options are enclosed. No open shelves for papers or stacks of documents on any tabletop.
- Declutter the entire room and especially the desk. I advise a telephone, computer and blotter, along with a single family photo, a pen and a book. That's it for the desktop.
- Dust that computer.
- Keep the décor in this room functional and professional, not comfy and casual.
- Add art and lighting in a variety of forms and applications for look and usability.
- Keep small office items and equipment in drawers or enclosed storage. No clutter on any visible surface.

- No toys or other children's items in this room, even if the little one likes to keep mommy or daddy company while they work.

Home Theatre and Media Room Staging

A home theatre or media room (same function, different name, basically) is a luxury asset in some properties and a liability in others. Never sacrifice space in a small to mid-sized home for a media room, unless the space is not useable for any other purpose. Doing so will present a "bachelor pad" atmosphere which is a turn-off to most buyers.

Larger homes which have a media rooms will please high-end real estate consumers, who expect top notch amenities from their properties. One thing is sure in all media room presentations: If you have the space, show it off and make sure that it shines! Here are some valuable tips for staging a home theatre:

- Inspect seating for wear and stains. Clean the upholstery or replace damaged seating surfaces.
- Do not get too "kitschy" with the theatre design. Watch taste-specific carpeting or too many "movie-

theatresque" furnishings. Make the room look casual, but not ridiculous.

- Of course, the heart of the room is the actual electronics. Make sure that these are up-to-date and operating perfectly. You want to blow buyers away, not make them think, "That's it, that's all there is?"
- Include a kitchenette if possible, complete with microwave, popcorn popper and refrigerator.
- Spend time designing the correct lighting for the room. Be sure to give the option of using the space for movie viewing with low indirect light, as well as other uses with normal interior lighting. Remote control lighting, with dimmers, is preferred.
- Media rooms work well in the basement, but can also be well suited to a converted accessible attic.

Basement Staging

Finished basements create valuable living space inside the home and offer other useful options, such as rental units and guest quarters. If your home has a finished basement, it is very wise to stage the rooms to maximize their appeal and usefulness, charming potential buyers in the process. If your basement is not finished, it is still important to make it as presentable and clean

clean as possible to prevent buyers from seeing it and running towards greener pastures.

Unfinished basements should be free from water and moisture issues, cracks in the foundation and any other problematic features. Make sure that access stairs are safe and in good repair. Also, look for options to improve slab or concrete flooring common in many unfinished spaces. A laminate floor is easy to lay down, making it a fast fix for ugly basement surfaces which are not prone to moisture. For a really fast fix, simply consider painting the floor for a fresh look and a bright appearance. *white — light bright uscafle*

Finished or unfinished basement spaces should always be tended to with loving care to make them as saleable as possible. Here are some excellent things to keep in mind when staging a basement: *428 Pinewood*

Put in door

- Add lighting to prevent the dark dingy environment common to subterranean rooms.
- Maximize natural light from any available windows by adding airy window treatments and trimming back surrounding exterior shrubbery.

little convenience

tear down window treatments + cut back shrubs

- An outside entrance to the basement is an asset, so be sure that if one is available, it is in good repair and access is unobstructed.
- Check all utility equipment for signs of damage or wear. Include the water heater, furnace, electrical panel and any indoor plumbing connections.
- Do not use unfinished spaces for clutter collection. Even if the space is not beautiful, at least get it organized and cleaned out.
- Check washer and dryer, if placed in the basement, to be sure they are operating correctly.
- Install or service dehumidifiers in moist basements to create a nicer and more livable atmosphere.
- If you do have water issues, solve them, don't cope with them or hide them.

Here are some staging tips exclusively for finished basements:

- Make the most of the available space. Try to set up multiple rooms if the layout allows. Typical uses for basement rooms include: family rooms, guest rooms, home offices and especially media rooms.
- Make small windows appear larger by hanging window treatments ceiling to floor. This will also make the ceiling appear taller.

- A summer kitchen is an asset and allows an easy conversion to a rental space. If you have an extra kitchen or bathroom in the basement, stage it to sell, just like your main kitchen and baths on the other levels of the home.

- Avoid open shelves for storage. This looks messy and junky. Instead, cleanout excess possessions and place them in storage. If this is not an option, try to use covered storage options instead.

- Finish the ceilings, as well as the walls. Beam ceilings with exposed wiring and pipes are always a big turn off for buyers. A few sheets of drywall or paneling will finish the space quickly and easily.

Attic Staging

Converted attic spaces add value to any home, while even unfinished attics can be selling points. Be sure to extend the staging project in your home to include all attic areas and you will certainly please buyers with the extra effort.

Unfinished attics are good for storage and non-traditional uses. Many people will convert attic space to suit their needs, without spending the time and money for professional grade renovations.

Some of the typical uses for attic space include: dark rooms, music rooms, meditation rooms and workshops. Even if you simply leave the space for storage, it is crucial to make it look useful and appealing.

In order to do enhance the space, clean out the area thoroughly and make sure there is solid flooring over the beams. Hide wiring and insulation using paneling or drywall and install some basic lighting fixtures. Adding shelving or covered storage options will make this space into a huge walk-in closet, which is always a buyer pleaser!

Here are a few suggestions for finished attic spaces:

- The main problem I see with finished attics is typically limited access by a ladder or steep pull-down stairway. Consider modifying tricky access points for a better functioning space.
- Attics make excellent extra bedrooms and home offices.
- Attics benefit from skylights, especially when natural light from windows may be limited or nonexistent.

Sunroom Staging

Enclosed sunrooms are a great way to welcome the outdoors into your home. Sunrooms come in a wide range of styles and applications and can be staged to fit many different room identities. The more functional your sunroom is, the more value it will add to your home.

Year-round sunrooms will be available for comfortable use all year long. This is common in warm climates and in colder climates when the room is fully insulated and heated. In many areas, "three season rooms" are popular and are fine for enjoying all types of weather, except the cold of winter. These rooms can often be converted to year-round use with some additional insulation and heating. However, this can be a pricey renovation in some cases.

In order to get the most bang for your buck when staging sunrooms, here are some tips of the trade to help:

- Define the space with an identity. It can be a home office, den or even a library. Do not just leave it as a "mystery room", since buyers will not know what to do with it any more than you do.

- Maximize the scenic views and access to the great outdoors. Keep window treatments airy and open, allowing more natural light and exterior vistas.
- Make sure the room has easy access to the yard and stage the surrounding exterior space to take advantage of the interior views. This will create a seamless transition to the welcoming atmosphere of the back or side yard.
- Keep colors in this room light and particularly neutral. This will invite the palate of nature to become the focal point in the room.
- Sunrooms make great places to house hot tubs and Jacuzzis, especially when the adjacent yard is well suited for entertaining.
- Look at the way in which the room joins into the main home. You will want to minimize evidence that this room may be an add-on. Check seams for cracks and inconsistencies and try to tie the interior of the sunroom to the nearby rooms of the main home using similar materials and décor features.
- Skylights are always nice in a sunroom.

Guest Room Staging

Dedicated guest quarters are a valuable luxury in any home. Having a guest room, or better yet, a guest house, is sure to have buyers particularly interested in purchasing the home. This is given the fact that these quarters are properly staged to add value and provide a warm and welcoming atmosphere which will create an emotional connection with buyers of all types.

Having a guest room is like a ringing endorsement for the size and functionality of your home. Space is obviously not limited, since you can put aside an entire room just for those special occasions in which you entertain overnight visitors. This speaks volumes to potential buyers who see this as a real asset. A guest house or suite is even better, since it will allow your guests to have a private bath and possibly even their own kitchen. This makes longer-term visitors feel at home, even if they are far away from their own house.

Here are some useful staging tips for preparing a guest room prior to placing your residence up for sale:

- Use basic bedroom staging techniques, but make the room particularly depersonalized and focused on presenting a luxury hotel room vibe.

- Increase this effect by providing a small refrigerator and a television contained in closed storage.
- Place art in the room which reflects travel.
- Make sure to lay out fresh towels and a robe, just as if you were actually expecting a guest.
- A welcome pillow on the bed is a nice touch, along with some hardcover books on the nightstand.
- Guest homes are often converted to rental units, so make sure to address this possibility in your staging, as well.

Garage Staging

The garage is the last area to discuss in the interior staging section. Garages play a larger role in prospective buyer's decision making processes than most sellers ever realize. Certain garage traits will really help to sell a home, while others will deter greatly from the chances for a speedy and top dollar offer.

Obviously, having a garage is an asset, while a car port is less so. Dedicated driveways or reserved parking spots are nice, but not as good as a garage. Not having any of these options can be a big deterrent to buyers, especially in areas with limited or no on-street parking generally available. However, the garage is about far more than just parking. It offers many other possibilities to various types of buyers.

Here are some factors to consider when staging the garage in a marketable home:

- Start on the outside. Make sure the doors work well and operate smoothly. Check them for aesthetic condition and repair or replace as needed.
- Plant some colorful flowers on the outside, near the entrance to the garage. You can use planting containers if flower beds are not available.
- Clean the garage out, including all the junk that was already in there when the home was first purchased. Throw away all those "projects" you have promised yourself to get to "someday". This junk collection is a huge liability.
- Illuminate the interior using a variety of lighting sources and try to maximize natural lighting if windows are available in the structure.
- Clean the floor with a pressure washer and finish it. That's right, finish it. Put down inexpensive garage flooring or simply paint the concrete for a nice look and a clean appearance.

- Pack up and store non-essentials and organize the few items you leave inside the garage with shelving or enclosed storage options.
- Keep the whole structure tidy. Clean out leaves, debris and cobwebs.
- If there is access directly to the house through the garage, make sure the path is unobstructed and the door is secure. This is a big selling point, especially for families.
- Do not waste space in large garages. Even if you only have one car, clean out the second spot to show the size and potential of the space.

Apartment, Loft and Townhouse Staging

There are a few special considerations for apartment type properties, such as condominiums, cooperatives, townhouses and loft spaces. Of course, all the regular rules of home staging still apply, but here are a few special considerations to include in your staging plan:

- Be sure to make potential buyers well aware of any public spaces and amenities offered by the building.

It is nice to take excellent pictures of these luxuries and make a collage inside your unit for all to see.

- Be sure to highlight available parking, especially reserved spaces in private garages.
- Allow buyers to see any additional storage space, if available.
- If you have a terrace, make sure to include the staging in the outdoor space, as well as the interior of the unit. Terraces with nice views can really bolster the asking price of a unit, so be sure to stage the area beautifully.
- Post information concerning maintenance fees and association fees in an easy to notice spot in the unit.

Staging Rentals

While home staging is used primarily for saleable properties, many landlords and management companies use the techniques as a means of making their rentals more appealing to high quality tenants. Staging rentals is exactly the same as staging for sales. Here are some points to consider about rental unit staging:

- Offering the unit furnished is a fantastic option. Typically the additional cost of a furnished unit will pay for all the décor within 12 to 24 months. After this time, it is all extra profit, month after month.

- Investing in quality furnishings is wise for landlords and managers. Even if the tenant does not need to rent the unit fully furnished, the items can be stored and used to stage unit after unit, as vacancies become available in this building.

- Staging helps prospective tenants see the usefulness and functionality in the rental's design and floor plan far better than an empty space could ever provide.

- Taking pictures of a furnished apartment will show much better in print and online ads. I know this from personal experience. I always advertise my rentals with fully furnished pictures and find the best tenants quickly time after time.

Commercial Property Staging

Staging commercial properties is another less common, but highly effective form of real estate marketing. Traditionally, commercial spaces are rented or sold, "as is"; empty and undecorated. A vacant commercial space is very difficult to envision as a functional business, so many potential tenants and buyers will pass up space after space looking for something which speaks to their emotions.

Staging a commercial space is not difficult to do. Generally it is easy to achieve a look and feel which will appeal to the target market. There are 3 primary ways to stage a commercial space, depending on the existing set-up and function of the space:

- Office staging is used for office space rentals and sales. These areas should be cleaned and set-up to resemble working office environments, complete with a reception area, work stations, mock computers and even a mock cafeteria. All the fixtures for this type of staging are cheap to rent or even buy, so there is little risk. However, the rewards of an excellent staging job can land you a sale or rental far faster and for a better asking price.
- Retail staging is used to set-up a mock retail establishment in a commercial space, including a cash register, customer service area, product racks and shelves and even fitting rooms or other useful areas. Retail staging will allow a variety of business owners to see how they can utilize the space to make their entrepreneurial dreams a reality.

- Restaurant staging is used in locations which are the site of a current or former eating establishment. Once set-up to house a restaurant business, the location becomes desirable for future eatery entrepreneurs, since much of the utility and infrastructure work is already done. Staging the space with a kitchen area, front desk, customer tables and chairs and even a bar is a fantastic way to attract quality and motivated buyers or renters to the location.

Commercial staging is a niche industry to be sure, but I have seen the demand for services grow steadily, year by year. In New York, where I live and work, commercial space is ultra-expensive and many quality spaces are fully staged when placed for sale or rental.

SECTION 4:

Exterior Home Staging

Outdoor Home Staging

In this section, I will cover many of the best strategies for improving the aesthetics of the outside of your home. When buyers first view your residence, they will immediately formulate an opinion of it. The presentation of your home is crucial from the first moment a potential buyer sees it. The appearance of the exterior of your home will set the emotional tone for the entire tour of your property.

Troublesome aesthetic or structural issues which become immediately obvious will really defeat all the good work you may have done throughout the home, so making a good first impression is absolutely vital. If the home looks warm and wonderful on the outside, there will be no shortage of prospective buyers making appointments to come see the inside...

Most of the exterior problems I see in many clients' homes are easy to rectify and do not involve spending much time or money. However, many sellers do not even recognize the problems with their curb appeal and therefore do not even think about ho solve them.

Remember to be objective when looking at your own property. Judge it just as a prospective buyer will see it as they pull up to view the home. Take in the entire way the home appears and then concentrate on each small facet of the property to create an idyllic environment which is sure to please even the most demanding buyers.

Front Yard Curb Appeal

The initial way in which a home is viewed by buyers as they arrive to tour the property is called curb appeal. Enhancing the curb appeal of your home is one of the most important criteria of your entire staging plan, so take the time and effort to do it right.

The home should be beautiful and in good repair, with proper landscaping and decorative touches to add interest, but not overwhelm. Here are many of the significant details which must be attended to during a curb appeal staging makeover:

ı at the street. Clean up the gutter in front of the

ᴮ ᵗᵒ

: and keep it neat and free from garbage,

ling water and other unaesthetic concerns.

- Is the sidewalk good repair? If not, patch cracks and level-out troublesome sections.
- The walkway to the front of your home should also be clean and free from debris or any weeds growing through the pavement or stones.
- The driveway should be in good condition and free from weeds, cracks and debris. A fresh coat of blacktop is an easy fix if the surface needs aesthetic help.
- Pressure washing all walkways can make them appear much newer. This is also a great way to remove oil stains from the driveway and garage interior.
- The garage doors should be clean and fresh looking.
- The actual exterior of the home should be in excellent repair, clean and pleasant. Repair any issues with exterior stucco, siding or paint. Double check the trim for rot and add a fresh coat of paint for a clean look.
- Inspect shutters and other types of external decoration. Additionally, inspect windows for any necessary repairs. Clean windows on the outside (and the inside, as well).

- Examine the roof for visual deformities or missing tiles. Also, make sure the gutters are installed property and not hanging or sagging. Be sure gutters are clean and not clogged. Check downspouts for proper drainage. If possible, remove old television antennas for an instant update to the home's appearance.

- Trim back overgrown foliage around the home. Never allow foliage to block windows or obscure large sections of the home. Remove dead trees and shrubs and replace with new landscaping features.

- Get the grass in good shape and keep it well groomed during the sales process. Many buyers find that hiring a landscaping professional is a good investment for maintaining a perfect lawn while the home is being actively shown.

- Plant fresh flowers around the house, with lots of color and texture. Concentrate on areas near the entrance to the garage, and of course, near the front door. Container planting is a good solution for homes without flower beds near ideal locations.

- Hide garbage cans in a dedicated shed. Never leave them visible, tucked on the side of the house or in the garage, if at all possible.

- No plastic lawn ornaments. High-end decorations are ok in small quantities, such as gazing globes or stone statues, but no garden gnomes or plastic flamingos anywhere.

- Consider revising boring or unappealing landscaping. A few hundred dollars can really transform the front of the home into a showplace, so this is a terrific investment which will return far more than the cost.

- Make sure fencing is in good repair and that gates open and shut properly.

- Set a lovely scene at the entrance to the home. If the property has a porch, stage it with some seating and a small table with a variety of colorful accents.

- Check the doorbell to insure proper function.

- Coordinate the mailbox, address numbers, outdoor lighting and any other features in the same style and color palate.

- Be sure there is adequate lighting on the outside of the home. Consider adding colored spotlights for a dramatic evening effect.

- Give the front door a fresh coat of paint in a welcoming color that contrasts with the palate of your home. Once again, I like red, hunter green, cottage blue or tudor brown.

- If you choose to put a wreath or other decoration on the front door, make it classy and made of natural materials. As always, nothing plastic.

Back Yard Staging

The back yard is a sanctuary of privacy and peace for many homeowners. It is a space to focus your staging efforts in order to create an atmosphere which will appeal to buyers of all types and preferences. While it is not possible to change the size or location of your yard, it is certainly possible to optimize the appearance and functionality, providing the home with added value and desirability.

Some yards are featureless, while others have specific details which make them even more useful. I will describe some general backyard staging strategies below and the specific feature tips in subsequent sections. Here are some excellent tips for preparing your back yard for sale:

- Start off by providing easy and unobstructed access to the yard from inside and outside of the home. Pay special attention to areas immediately visible or accessible from the home interior. A welcoming environment visible outside will draw buyers to investigate the lovely yard.

- Inspect fencing for defects or areas which may require repair. Pay special attention to gates.

- Keep the grass green and healthy. Many home sellers enlist professional landscaping help to make their lawn and garden shine while actively marketing their property. This is a small investment for an impressive result.

- Plant colorful flowers in containers or flower beds.

- Remove dead foliage, trees and shrubs and replace with nice new landscaping items. Try to maximize privacy, without compromising yard space. This can be accomplished with tall, narrow trees and bushes or an easy-to-grow natural screen, such as bamboo.

- Keep toys and garden implements off the lawn and stored properly in a dedicated shed. Enlist the kids to help out in staging and maintaining the back yard.

- Water features create tranquility in yards which suffer from background noise, such as that from main roads, highways, industrial or commercial installations or railroads.

- If you have a guest house, cottage, pool, patio or deck, see the sections below for specific details on staging these individual spaces. Do not neglect these valuable assets by failing to perform your home staging throughout the entire property.

Staging Decks and Patios

An outdoor deck or patio should be staged as an extension of the overall living space, not just a limited-use property feature. In order to do this, set the tone using these design guidelines:

- Inspect lumber or pavers for wear and tear and replace as needed. Be sure to double check railings, banisters and stairs for safety issues.
- Try to provide a mixture of sun and shade on a deck or patio for maximum functionality. Sun can be maximized by cutting back trees in the yard, while shade is easy to achieve with foliage, a pergola or large free-standing umbrellas.
- Select patio and deck furniture to suit the proportions of the space, not the property owner's actual needs. Remember this is staging.
- Always set the table and chairs as if you were expecting guests for a special affair. Use double-sided tape or Velcro to secure items to the table. Set plates, glasses, flowers and silverware for a lovely garden

party atmosphere which is guaranteed to please buyers.

- Use containers for flower and herb planting on the deck or patio.
- Be sure that entry points to the home are working well and are unobstructed for easy access.
- Inspect the deck or patio area for bugs and signs of insect activity or infestation.
- Exterior lighting is more than functional; it should also be festive and versatile for any occasion.
- Clean the barbeque grill or hide it completely with a brand new opaque cover.
- If you have an outdoor kitchen, inspect appliances, countertops, seating and fixtures for proper function and operation. Repair or replace items as needed. Do not forget to double check electrical and plumbing connections.

Staging Pools

Inground pools are assets for many properties, while above ground pools can be seller liabilities. If you have a beautiful inground pool, stage it right to help sell your home. If you have an above ground, do your best to maximize its appeal and minimize liabilities associated with these structures or consider dismantling it altogether for an easy fix. Here are some basic pool staging considerations:

- First off, make sure the pool is immaculately clean if it is open and in use, or closed and covered properly, if it is not.
- Be sure that your have adequate safety features in place, such as fencing and a cover to prevent mishaps with pets and young children.
- Use outdoor lighting to provide mood enhancement. Lighting can really be incredibly beautiful when designed around the effect of a pool or pond.
- Check pool heaters, pumps and filters to insure that they are working correctly.
- Check access ladders, slides and diving boards for safe operation and a secure fit.
- Use water-hardy containers with flowers near the pool for a delightful natural look. Better yet, use masonry and landscaping to provide an organic "grotto" look to your pool or spa.
- Hot tubs and spas should also be checked for proper operation, electrical connections and cleanliness.

SECTION 5:

Home Staging Checklist

Home Staging Checklist

I know there is a lot to remember when considering staging your home. I am including this checklist which covers many of the tips, strategies and details applicable to most properties and rooms in you home. Some of these are review points from previous sections, while others may be new to you:

- Choose the best staging method for you, be it DIY or full service using a professional stager.
- For DIYers, do not be afraid to hire a staging consultant to assist you with planning your project.
- Declutter and depersonalize everything.
- Organize the remaining furnishings and possessions.
- Experiment with several furniture placements to optimize available interior space.
- Clean everything inside and out.
- Rent a storage space for extra items which can not remain in the home. Alternately, have a garage sale to sell these items or donate them to charity.
- Always think about form and function.

- Define an obvious and recognizable purpose for every room in your home. No multipurpose rooms.
- Maintain the staging design by inspecting the home prior to showings and open houses.
- Get the whole family involved in the staging plan for maximum cooperation and effect.
- Utilize rental services for furniture, art and tools.
- When buying items for staging, keep the cost minimal, since these are merely fixtures, not items needed to provide years of use. Try to make more than buy.
- Always view the property through the eyes of a demanding, critical buyer. Look for problems!
- Do not be offended or bothered by changing the home décor. Staging does not mean that the seller has bad taste. It just means that a less taste-specific environment will appeal to more buyers.
- Find creative ways to improve the existing furniture and fixtures. New paint and hardware can update almost anything.
- Less is more. Do not over-decorate. Remove rather than add when it comes to furniture.
- Float furniture. Do not limit it to lining the walls.
- Clean windows inside and out.
- No heavy draperies or curtains. Keep window treatments light and airy to maximize natural light.

- Utilize dimmers to create mood lighting.
- Add new electric socket and light switch cover plates for a fresh, clean look.
- Don't forget to stage the closets.
- Clean carpets and rugs with professional equipment.
- Keep the design of the home cohesive.
- No plastic anything.
- No wallpaper or borders.
- No collections of family photo galleries.
- No dusty blinds. Better yet, no plastic or aluminum blinds altogether.
- Arrange accessories in like colors or textures in groups of 3's and 5's.
- No burned-out light bulbs anywhere.
- Keep vigilant for household odors, including pets, cigarettes and cooking. If you can't smell them, get help from someone who is brutally honest.
- All lights should be on when showing the home, even during the daytime. Add lighting, as needed.
- Stage the entire property, inside and out.
- Minimize items on any furniture tops or counter tops.
- No magnets, photos or notes on the refrigerator.
- Never leave rooms empty.

- Be aware of the temperature in your home when receiving buyers. Make them comfortable at all costs. If they are too hot or too cold, they will not buy the home.
- Keep your receipts. Remember, property staging is tax deductible.
- Appeal to all 5 senses in every room of the home: Sight, touch, sound, taste and smell.
- If your staging job is so good that it makes you reconsider selling your home, then you have done an excellent job!

SECTION 6:

Home Staging Career

Home Staging Career

I get many letters from readers who enjoyed this book and would like more information about a career as a professional home stager. I have written a tremendous amount of material on my website about beginning a real estate staging career and all the training which is beneficial.

If the idea of working as a property stager appeals to you, I highly recommend you investigate your educational options, as this is an exciting and fast-paced industry which is currently enjoying fantastic expansion and growth.

As a home stager, you have many work opportunities available to you. You can be your own boss and begin your own staging company. You can work for an existing staging firm as an intern, assistant or full stager. You can work for a real estate office, as an in-house stager or consultant. You can work for a property management company, staging model units or rental apartments. You can work for a decorator as a home stylist. You can work for a furniture rental supplier, providing staging help for clients. You can even work in many retail niches, especially

118

n the furniture sector. There are just so many avenues available to qualified property stagers. The very best staging experts can even make their way to television stardom on one of the many programs featuring real estate staging in action.

Home Stager Training

Stagers can succeed no matter how much or how little education they have in formal property enhancement. In fact, some of the most successful stagers have never taken a formal course and many made their way to the top long before formal staging courses even existed.

However, I always recommend education as a great tool towards success in all endeavors and home staging is no exception to this rule. The more you know, the better prepared you will be to deal with any circumstance that may arise in your professional career. The acquisition of knowledge is never a waste of time or money. That being said, there is no reason why an aspiring stager can not get started without any formal classroom training, especially if they can nail down an internship with a successful company that will train them for free, on the job.

For aspiring stagers that are interested in formal training there are many choices available, ranging in value and price considerably. Online courses and mail-order courses are often less expensive, but lack the hands-on experience of real classroom or on-the-job training.

Given the potentially high cost of formal schooling, it might be best to seek an unpaid internship and do everything possible to distinguish yourself to get a paid job upon completion of your training. At least this path will provide practical experience and will not cost anything, besides your time. As an added benefit, you will make great industry connections and if you can stand out with superior skills, you will almost certainly move into a compensated position quickly.

Be wary of high-priced training courses that promise the world, but have no way to possibly deliver. For example, some training companies promise a job to successful graduates of their costly education program. The problem is that the training costs thousands of dollars and the job pays minimum wage, often requiring working at odd hours and in less than ideal conditions. Not exactly a dream job, by most people's standards...

I have actually received many letters from graduates of such programs who told me that they learned more from this very book than they did from their combined "training and employment" at some scam companies. It is sad, so buyers always beware...

If you are going to pay for expensive training, be sure that you are receiving it from a respected and reputable source. This source should be accredited by a respected and reputable agency.

Most importantly, graduation should allow you to take an exam to become certified by a particular governing body. This way, you will officially be a certified home stager, with a worthwhile credential. Being certified by a company or association with a poor reputation is actually an impediment to a future career, so choose your training wisely.

Home Staging Career Facts

Stagers do not need to be licensed. They do not need to be certified. In fact, there are no requirements for calling yourself a stager and performing job functions in any legal capacity. That being said, there are guidelines that all aspiring stagers should always follow when offering services on their own:

- Always maintain adequate business insurance and bonding, as needed. This will protect you from all manner of liabilities, including litigation, property damage and professional problems of all sorts.

- Do not accept jobs that are beyond your ability, budget or capacity to fulfill. This can only ruin your reputation, which is a difficult thing to repair, once it becomes tarnished.

- Always be honest and ethical. Although this seems like it should be a given, I am surprised how many people do not keep this golden rule in mind during everything they do in life.

- Consider joining a home stager association, such as The International Association of Home Staging Professionals, The American Society of Home Stagers and Redesigners, or The Real Estate Staging Association. These organizations provide many support services that you will find helpful as your career flourishes.

Home Staging Career Tools

There are many tools that might come in handy during a career in home staging. However, few are actually inherent to performing the job well and many can be purchased for a few dollars at the local store. Below, I have listed all the things you will absolutely need or want to get in order to start a staging career in aspect of the business:

- A measuring tape is crucial. It is like air to a home stager; you just can't live without it. Measurement is very important in all staging plans. You need to know the size of every area in order to find suitable furnishings and maintain a sense of ideal proportion.

- Furniture gliders are small devices used for moving heavy furniture around easily and without damaging the floor surface. They are cheap and easy to use. A normal person can easily move a full size piece of furniture alone when using gliders.

- Pen and paper must always be handy to chart down measurements and take notes. Do not rely on your memory, since there will be too many details to accurately remember.

- Basic tools, such as power and manual screwdrivers, hammers, saws, wrenches, staplers and sanders, are certainly very useful.

- Painting supplies should always be on hand.

- Various types of tape, in a selection of colors, will serve many purposes.

- Plastic ties are ideal for securing wires, fabric and other objects.

- Color palate tools and shade samples should be available in abundance.

- Graph paper is excellent for making 2 dimensional scale models and room representations. Simply create an accurate scale (1 square = 1 foot) and cut out all the furniture items from colored paper. Then place and arrange the items on your graph, which represents the size and shape of the actual room. This is incredibly useful for planning large or busy spaces.

- A laptop computer or tablet can perform a world of staging tasks, from organizing the project to real time 3 dimensional modeling and color palate selection. There is advanced home staging software available which is simply amazing.

Home Staging Career Advice

Finally, in closing out this primer on home staging, I want to offer some advice based on my years of working successfully in several facets of the real estate sector. These pointers will help novice and aspiring stagers to get their businesses off to a good start and will set the stage for years of financial rewards in an exciting and rewarding career path:

- First and foremost, before going into business, be sure to write and revise a thorough business plan. The reason why most new companies fail is because they did not have a concrete blueprint for success from day one. When it comes to making it in a competitive industry, you can not just "play it by ear".

- Never forget that you can offer both home staging and home styling in order to maximize your customer base.

Be flexible with your services and encourage repeat styling clients with discounts and special rates.

- Don't even think about a career in home staging unless you already have or are willing and able to make the connections you will need to succeed. You must actively network with area real estate professionals, real estate attorneys, furniture rental companies, property management agencies, and of course, potential clients.

- When you are just starting out, be sure to offer some free work, or at least deeply discounted work, to get people to try your services. Make sure to over-deliver on results, even if you are working for free and even spending a bit of money to get the job done. This small investment of time and money will pay great dividends if you can impress new clients and earn paid referrals.

- Offer clients ongoing incentives to recommend you, at any time in the future. Build a phone and email list of contacts and market to these people regularly, but not annoyingly. Be sure to ask each new client who referred them to you and reward the referrer handsomely.

- Most importantly, take lots and lots of pictures and video of your work and always improve your portfolio. Pictures sell jobs more than your words ever could, so really invest time and effort into visually representing your staging in the best light possible.

TERMS OF USE